FLIPPING THE SWITCH

FLIPPING THE SWITCH

Strategies for

Expanding Your Business Online

by Chris Heller

Copyright © 2013

All rights reserved. No part of this publication may be reproduced or transmitted in any form or by any means, electronic or mechanical, including photography, recording, or any information storage and retrieval system, without the prior written permission of the publisher.

TABLE OF CONTENTS

Introduction 1
Chapter 1
    Changes 3
Chapter 2
    Who am I? 7
Chapter 3
    Getting Ready 14
Chapter 4
    How Do I Look? 19
Chapter 5
    The Subliminal World 23
Chapter 6
    Perspective 34
Chapter 7
    Adding the Numbers 42
Chapter 8
    What's on the Shelf? 48
Chapter 9
    Selling Information 54
Chapter 10
    Who Will Wear the Hats? 57
Chapter 11
    Outsourcing: The Workforce that Never Stops 62
Chapter 12
    Good Will Hunting 65
Chapter 13
    The Power of the Sequential Subconscious 71

INTRODUCTION

These are exhilarating times.

You may live seven lifetimes and never see this sort of potential in the business world again. History is filled with great businessmen; Marco Polo, Christopher Columbus, Ray Kroc, Steve Jobs. What did they have in common? They chose a different path…a side door…and they made up their own rules. They seized opportunity.

In the mid-90s, the Internet was just such an opportunity. Investors ran across university campuses, throwing millions at anyone who knew a bit from a byte. The result was occasional galactic success, but more often than not, it was simply poorer investors.

Why? The investors were gambling on being the fastest wagons in the Oklahoma land rush. The result was the same; the wagons of prospective land barons broke down, horses went lame and murders settled ownership of property claims. When the dust settled, it was the merchants who sold food, lantern fuel and new wagon wheels who reaped the profits.

In the early days a domain name cost $50 and the state of Michigan spent more than a million dollars to have their website built. Today you can get a domain for three bucks and the Michigan.gov website ranks as one of the most inefficient, confusing and ugly sites among the U.S. fifty. A 10-year-old kid with a smart phone could build a better site.

The lesson here? Pack fifty shovels in the back and ignore the guys with black hats. There is money to be made and there are empires waiting to be built. When you finish this book you will be inspired and savvy enough to know whom to trust. It's time for someone new.

CHAPTER 1

Changes

It was 1819—almost 200 years ago, and ESCP, the first business college in the world opened in Paris, France. In the following years, the names became legendary; Wharton School in 1881, Harvard Business School in 1908 and The Thunderbird School of Global Management, an institute focusing on global business in 1946, are but a few. It was as recently as 1998 that Wharton launched its Wharton Research Data Services in its new Computing and Information Technology department. Babies born in that year are only now 15 years-old.

The point here is that anyone reading this book will have grown up in the pre-Internet world. Certainly any initial formal education did not include technology. The Internet's effect on business cannot be underestimated. Let's look at just a few of the key areas.

Terminology

We have become a worldwide society of acronyms. Do you speak Internet-ese? Do you know when to use a .gif, a

.png or to go full out for .jpg? Can you use a .swf on your website and is it viewable on every platform, including tablets? Are you comfortable chatting in HTML 5 or are you still scraping together functionality in HTML 4? Do you know the difference between an iBook and an eBook?

The 2012 word of the year was "hashtag." If you think this is drug-related, you should probably read the rest of this book before you attend that next dinner party. Don't look now, but this is the language of the Internet and they're speaking it from China to Brazil. More the point, when you wake up in the morning, it's likely a new "word" will have been born overnight and you'll need to know it as well.

Customers

There was a time when these folks walked in your front door and lived in town with their kids, who grew up and became your new customers. You knew their birthdays, grieved with them when they lost Grandma and handled your business with integrity because they knew where you lived.

Today it's a little different. Thanks to the Internet, you have the opportunity to expand your business beyond those who arrive in a car or on foot. You have the entire world, and in some cases, beyond. That space station floating around out there was partially built in Russia. Did you think the space station wasn't connected to the Net? Tell that to the astronauts who tweeted their presence from the station in early 2010. Where there are consumers, there is business.

Education

The foundations of business have always included a solid university education. In fact, you would be hard pressed to land even an entry-level job without some acronyms behind your name.

This, too, has changed and you can reference one particular set of billionaires—those who dropped out of college. They include Bill Gates, Mark Zuckerberg, Gabe Newel and the late Steve Jobs. Why did they drop out? It was because college was holding them back. The Internet changes at such a pace that you cannot complete a technology-based class before it has changed yet again.

How do you compete? How do you keep up? You have to live it. You have to a) understand where it is now, b) understand how it relates to your business and to your customers and c) once you understand it completely, you have to become an innovator.

Transparency

Once all the terminology rolls off your tongue like a respectable geek, you still need to relate to your customer and in today's world of business, that means that your customers run your business. On a personal level, everything you or your key employees do is trackable on the Net. That TGIF party when you drank a little too much and un-buttoned your shirt to your naval will be making headlines on Facebook by Saturday morning. Customers cannot only find your company on Google maps, they can find your house inside those gated walls as well. You may think you can confound that disgruntled customer with a maze of automated telephone menu selections but he will be ringing your cell phone on the nightstand at 3 a.m. if you're not careful.

But, on the other hand, that transparency is available for your use as well. For absolutely no cost whatsoever Google will share with you enough analytics and trending terminology to allow you to build an entire business concept around a single search term. What this means is that you don't need to spend millions of dollars for a shotgun Super Bowl ad—you can achieve greater market share for your cola by targeting the competition's customers, and converting them. That's one of those important terms, by the way…conversion. It no longer means recruiting for the Jehovah's Witness or dragging a drinker to an AA meeting. It's about turning a simple Google search into a sale for your product.

Feeling a little off-balance? That's fine. You've come to the right place. We're going to cover concepts to creation and when you're done, you'll have a much firmer handle on what you can do to harness this immeasurable power for your own business growth.

CHAPTER 2

Who Am I?

So, you've decided to evaluate taking your company onto the great Internet grid. This can be a huge decision for some companies, and not so big for others. Let's take a look at some examples.

John is self-employed and paints houses. He is a third-generation painter, having apprenticed with both his grandfather and years later, his father. He inherited his father's clients and a good deal of equipment and while today fewer houses need painting, John is determined to maintain the family business.

Urged on by his son, John is considering having a website built. He spent several weekends at the local library honing his computer skills and recently bought a modest used computer for his home. Translating his business, which is purely service-oriented in a local market, to the expansion possibilities the Internet provides, was his first objective.

John began by evaluating his competition. He searched for "house painters" using his local zip code and discovered that about half of his competitors already had functioning sites. He noted they also happened to be the same companies who were considered still viable in his otherwise dwindling industry. Common sense told him this was no accident.

Most of these companies had what could be considered a business card site, meaning that they simply had a presence that included their contact information and a Google map showing their location. This, at least, made them searchable by Google and included them when a homeowner was sourcing painters using the computer.

One company, however, caught John's eye. Prominently on their home page they displayed a slide show presentation of homes they had painted; wisely displaying both 'before' and 'after' pictures side by side. John spent more time at this site than the others and evaluated the slideshow as though he were a potential customer himself.

John engaged the services of a web designer and in their first meeting, the designer asked him a pointed question. "What makes you different from your competition?" John pondered the question a few minutes, remembering the business card sites and then, the company with the slideshow. He showed the designer that site and remarked how much he liked the slideshow. The designer repeated his question.

John responded, "I'm a third generation painter. I've painted houses that my father previously painted, and his father before him. You can't stay in business that long if you don't know what you're doing."

The designer nodded and then asked, "What has three generations of painting taught you?"

John thought a few moments and answered, "It's all about the preparation. A successful job depends on the prep you're willing to do. The paint lasts longer and the finished job looks better."

The designer then asked, "Would you say that you specialize in one thing more than another?"

John answered, "Oh, that's easy. Historic homes…espe-

cially those on the Historic Register. There are a lot of details you have to follow in order to comply with their requirements. Colors, detailing, even the type of paint. It has to be very historically accurate. In fact, my customers demand these details because they get a healthy tax break for doing so and that helps to offset the cost of maintenance." John sat back proudly and the designer nodded, taking notes.

Two weeks later John met with the designer again who unveiled a site design he'd created for John. There on the home page was a graphic collage. It showed one of the historic homes John had recently finished and John's picture was superimposed in a feathered box beside it. Behind these were two images; an identical presentation of his father and the same house he'd completed 30 years earlier, and then another with his grandfather and the same house 20 years prior to that. Below the images sat the bold head, "We've painted this historical beauty for three generations. Check back in 40 years to see why."

With that message John's company was separated from the competition and people associated him with enduring history and preservation. His message was so strong that he began to get inquiries from customers in distant states. Three years later John expanded his business to two locations; one in the Midwest and one in the Deep South, taking advantage of the opposing climates and he began painting year-round. Thus, John expanded to two states, using the Internet as his bridge.

* * *

So, in this above scenario, the owner, John, was thorough in his information gathering by checking out his competition, but his designer helped him with the more critical perspective; namely what set him apart from his competition. In business parlance this is what is called a USP, or unique selling proposition. Essentially – it's what John offered to his customer that convinced them he was unique.

He was able to visit his competition's sites and become a potential customer—something he would not be able to accomplish in reality. Naturally his competition would never make a bid for John's business or reveal their techniques in attracting new customers. At the same time, John had the very unique opportunity to show up his competition by using the three-generation advantage; something he would have been unlikely to "sell" in a face-to-face or telephone conversation with a potential client.

John also joined a whole new echelon of companies across the U.S. He became known for his painting and restoration of historical properties and had the actual family history to prove he knew what he was doing.

By forcing John to examine his business as a potential customer, he strengthened his self-identification and then was able to encapsulate it, creating an opportunity to move beyond his local area. This was a concept this local house painter never even considered.

In a product-based business, the "Who Am I?" question may be easier to resolve. Most retailers face competition that is far more quantitative; how much does it cost? If you sell a Sharp 42" flat screen television, it's fairly easy for customers to compare you to other companies who carry the identical product. Smaller, hometown television stores may resist this shopper comparison, knowing their steeper overhead will make their prices noticeably higher and customers, including those who are currently patrons, may look to the big box stores to get a better deal. They may feel they have a better chance of making the sale if the customer walks into their store and they're able to use a first-name sales approach. However, they are overlooking one huge advantage they have; they are local and therefore the customer can get instant gratification.

When Mr. Smith's tube television blanks out two hours before the big game, he's not going to shop Amazon; he's going to shop local and he will be interested in upgrading his set to a nice big flat screen. The hometown store needs to have an online presence so that Mr. Smith is aware that the store is open, has the selection and the customer service to get that new set installed. The hometown store may also deliver and will know the local cable box hook-ups so they will have the right HDMI cable with them. When Mrs. Smith's refrigerator no longer keeps the milk cold, where is she going to turn? To the local store where she knows she can hand over a credit card and they'll take care of the rest—including hauling away the old unit.

* * *

The lesson here is that while the local store may feel they aren't competitive; they actually have an advantage, but must have an online presence to be considered.

When was the last time you looked up a business in the Yellow Pages? If you're like most people, you have a smart phone or laptop that is easier to find and faster to access. If you use your smart phone, you only need to click on the phone number and the phone dials itself. The days of yellow tomes piling up in the hall closet are soon over. So ask yourself; will you hide your business in the hall closet or give it the convenience of click-button access?

Let's move up the scale a bit to the corporation who already enjoys a national customer base. They may have an existing ad agency or in-house marketing staff that handles catalog distribution, as well as follow-up sales calls from territory reps. While it makes perfect sense to cut the cost of those catalogs, transitioning customer expectation may have you a bit concerned.

Studies show that the most successful companies online have an accompanying brick and mortar location as well.

Kenna Art is housed in an industrial park and employs about 30 people. It acts as a distributor for multiple lines of fine art supplies including paints, brushes, canvases, craft wood and paint cleaning chemicals. It has both retail and individual customers. Kenna has grown quickly and has relied completely upon its 80-page catalog, printed on newsprint and mailed out on a yearly basis. Kenna maintains two full-time artists on staff whose job it is to paint examples using their products and provide input on the best companies to represent.

Kenna's account manager has convinced the CEO to put the company online, expanding their current business card site to one that is fully-equipped for e-commerce. The site features how-to videos demonstrating painting techniques by the staff artists and displays all the product lines in blazing color. This alone made the black-and-white newsprint catalog appear outdated and cheap—although the postage needed was anything but. Individuals who visit the site are able to see the how-to videos, order supplies at retail pricing and download painting patterns. Retail customers see a different version of the site and are able to order supplies at wholesale pricing—but more importantly, Kenna allows them to enjoy a branded duplicate of the Kenna site that lets retailers refer their customers but get credit for the sale.

This option was so attractive that numerous small retailers chose to use Kenna's referral site rather than build their own. The result is that Kenna has gained retail, as well as individual, customers and their mailing list has skyrocketed.

Kenna has converted much of their sales staff to fielding in-house customer service calls, which cut their travel expenses. Their growth has also encouraged them to branch out from the painting supplies and they have begun to stock additional crafting materials such as clays, beads, yarns, scrapbooking and stamps.

Kenna's paper catalog has been replaced by a full-color PDF with embedded order form. Now they need not wait a whole year to introduce new products and can advertise sales directly via email on a weekly and monthly basis.

Warehousing and shipping have been vastly improved as these systems became automated and the customer keys in the ordering information rather than a Kenna sales rep.

Lastly, Kenna's growth and automation has made them a more viable concern and they are able to command better wholesale pricing and are now invited to carry selective product lines that were formerly not available to them. They've developed a cooperative relationship with a similar company in England and now enjoy international distribution.

* * *

While these examples of how companies of any size can take advantage of an online presence, these are only three of millions of similar stories. Business has changed across the planet and whether you feel it's a positive thing or not, you can no longer afford to sit by the side and criticize. You are only aiding in your own obsolescence.

Chapter 3

Getting Ready

Although you might find the thought of expanding your company on the Internet intimidating, you may be surprised when you discover that it's the best thing you have ever done.

It is not unlike moving into a new house. When you're in the planning stages you go through all the corners and stacks of things you've accumulated over the years. You generally decide most of it is obsolete—so you get rid of it. You prioritize the items that need to go at the door of the moving truck so you can get to it quickly. You strategize the route you will drive to your destination and calculate how many people will be needed when and where to accomplish the goal. You transfer utilities and leave a forwarding address. A new bank account is established, you will need to find a new doctor and school and choose the colors of your brand new furnishings. Most importantly, you let your friends and family know where to find you in the future.

What do I need to expand on the Net?

One of the first things to consider is your goal. Begin by asking yourself these questions:

- Am I duplicating my brick and mortar or creating an entirely new arm of my existing business?
- Am I hoping to attract more customers to my brick and mortar or do I want to sell/service them online?
- What advantages can the Internet provide that my brick and mortar doesn't offer?
- Who is my competition currently; who will it be online and what do they offer the customer?
- Who is my ideal customer and what are they looking for?

While these are only a few of the questions you will have to consider, they are the basic preliminaries to get you started.

Let's consider Question 1. It may not be as simple as it first looks. There are opportunities opened by a website that you may not have even considered. For example, Walmart, the mega-discount retailer has roughly 4,000 stores in the U.S. as of this writing. Add to that another 6,000 internationally and one might wonder why the retailer would even bother with an online presence. After all, there's one within driving distance of almost any city in the U.S.

Take a moment, however, to look at their website. Walmart is notorious for maximizing the profit in every square inch of its stores—but consider that online their "floor" space is essentially unlimited. If you wanted to buy a bed mattress, would Walmart be the first place you would look? Probably not—you would opt for a mattress or furniture store because when a consumer thinks of a Walmart store, they envision shelves of smaller items; not aisles stacked with mattresses. And yet, on walmart.com you can order any variety of mattresses and enjoy free shipping to your door. Not even the local furniture store is likely to include free delivery. So the magic here is the consumer's expectation of receiving Walmart's storied lowest prices possible and getting their new mattress delivered to the door at no additional charge. How convenient is this for people who happen to drive a VW bug?

Hence, some of Walmart's products cannot be found in their brick and mortar stores; they are found online only. How would this work for your business? If you were suddenly given unlimited "floor" space, would you carry more products or offer additional services? Could you establish a manufacturer relationship with "just in time delivery" so that if you sold 10,000 mattresses, as example, the first day you wouldn't need to warehouse these, but could have them shipped directly from the manufacturer?

It's not difficult to envision that your entire business model can be changed with this concept. If your customer base online exceeds your local base ten-fold, you would, indeed, begin to structure your business for the online customer almost exclusively, especially if your online overhead was negligible. Keep in mind that Walmart's well-publicized strong-arm buying practices are based on having those 6,000 retail stores; but they only have one store online. Thus, in an online sense, you would be just as big as Walmart. What sort of possibilities does that offer?

In Question 2 we look at the purpose of your online expansion. Do you strictly wish to only deal face-to-face with your customers or can you accomplish this in a virtual world? Naturally this depends on the business. If you are an orthodontist, there is little for you to offer online, so a business card site is appropriate; just enough for people using the Internet rather than the Yellow Pages to find you. But even if you sell doughnuts, if they become popular, UPS delivers anywhere overnight.

Question 3 may seem a repeat of the aforementioned strategies, but it can also be a bit different. When we refer to advantages, we mean opportunities that weren't necessarily open to you offline. Let's say you are an artist with a small studio and you would like to offer classes to budding painters. Your studio may not accommodate the space needed for this—where an online video course in a membership site could.

Perhaps you would like to employ handicapped workers who cannot come in to your office each day, but they are able to work from home with a computer. Your website need not be consumer-related; it can be an online office where your employees are able to interact with you and the rest of your staff. There are any number of advantages to having a "rubber-band staff" that allows you to enlist the help of more people when needed, but otherwise maintain a consistently low employee overhead.

Moving on to Question 4 and examining that your competition's use of the Internet can have some bearing on your decision. That said, it's important that you not rely solely on the others to structure your use. If you spend all your time watching them, you will find yourself running their business and yours will be identical. Where's the advantage in that?

Much of this comes with the analysis of who the competition actually is. If your business happens to sell tires, locally they would be the other tire retailers or perhaps stores like Sears or Walmart. In that scenario it's easy to compare the advantages you offer to theirs. Are you willing to provide roadside service for a flat tire? Perhaps you have negotiated contracts with area used car dealers to refit trade-ins with new tires while it's being detailed.

When you move that tire business online, however, you'll be up against every tire retailer on the Internet (assuming the tires are shipped to the customer.) What does the online competition offer? Do they offer free installation at a participating dealer or a lifetime guarantee? Will they ship the tires for free?

This brings us to Question 5 and a discussion of what the customer will be looking for. As in the previous examples, your local customer and your Internet customer are quite different. It's not only a matter of accessibility, nor is it a matter of simply having more online customers. It is more about having the right customers. This speaks to the business adage of not trying to be everything to everyone. For example, you may have a service where you offer customized motorcycles. This can be a fairly high-ticket service and in order to do this locally, you may be forced to offer general motorcycle repair; just to keep the doors open. This prevents you from doing what you do best, and what you love—namely, custom design. In an online world you can attract specific customers—those who share your love of the craftsmanship, as well as the sport, and who have the income to indulge in your services. It won't take too many of those to let you lock the front door and turn up the speakers as you immerse yourself in what is now a studio environment that makes your heart sing as you awaken each morning. In short, the Internet could be the answer to your life's dream.

Many companies find that when they analyze the sort of questions listed above, they find the need to re-align their business model. It can force them to recognize low-profit areas and how they can reverse that trend or possibly abandon it altogether. This sort of housecleaning points out weaknesses in your system; it may be that your customer service needs improvement, that your shipping costs are too high or that you should maintain a more flexible inventory that answers demand. Ask yourself whether you are serving your customer's needs or forcing them to swallow what you happen to sell. In doing so, are you simply creating new customers for your competition?

Chapter 4

How Do I Look?

When your business is located on the corner or in an industrial park, the outward appearance has a direct impact on how your customers will perceive you. Depending on what you offer, that appearance may actually influence not just your reputation, but your sales and your ability to overcome the competition.

One example of this could be a furniture store. A customer who walks into a warehouse environment with furnishings stacked in metal racks expects lower prices since the aesthetics have been minimalized. Likewise if your store occupies an entire block and the ceiling is glaring with fluorescent lights while huge orange sale posters obliterate your windows, he expects that you have massive buying power and are probably selling products that are intended to be replaced in five years. If, however, that customer walks into your store and finds it to be a well-landscaped brick building with arched, leaded-glass doors and the interior is subtly lit with furniture grouped in tasteful vignettes, he will perceive that what you sell will be expensive. He will be less likely to try and bargain with you and will actually assume an air of being accustomed to the finer things in life. He will expect your fabrics to be custom-ordered and that the construction will guarantee the pieces he buys from you may be handed down through the family. He will understand that local delivery is included in the price, there are no warehouse sales and your "scratch and dent" pieces are shipped to the econo-retailer. This sort of store represents a long-term relationship with its customers and the sales representatives remember their customers' names and which pieces they've already purchased.

Where does your business fit into that picture? How do you differentiate yourself online from your competition in that same way?

There is no brick for the building, no subtle lighting and no exclusive shopping district. You cannot remember peoples' names when you cannot see them.

While the answer is not as obvious as you might think, there are, indeed, methods to accomplish your goal. They simply require an adaptation of the visual concepts you've already come to know.

It is interesting to note, however, that some retailers who considered their customers a select group have branched beyond that to take advantage of a more multi-tiered customer pool.

Moving back to the furniture store example…the huge discount store will also have a huge parking lot. This is intended to suggest that they are used to being the focus of large crowds, intent upon capitalizing on a deeply-discounted sale for a limited time. Big parking lots = crowds expected = great deals that last for a short time. Customers are treated in an assembly-line process.

Tasteful stores with smaller parking lots suggest intimacy, enduring relationships, exclusivity. They offer one handicapped parking space as opposed to thirty; there is no room to park a motorhome and no loading dock where you can back up your pickup or tie the new sofa on the roof of your minivan.

How would you translate that sort of intimacy to an online presence? Consider when a customer arrives at your site that your products (in this case furniture) are grouped according to manufacturer or style, and not just listed "sofas" or "beds" as you would find in a discounter. This immediately tells the customer they should recognize a brand; like the name and year of a fine wine. If they don't, they're probably in the wrong place.

If that customer were to search for "Lazyboy" let's say, you might carry the same recliner as the discounter but when the results page displays, there are only two recliners pictured. One is in leather and one is in polished cotton. The price is not prominent, but the swatches of other fabrics, are. This tells the customer they can't just load their pickup at the dock; this is a custom-order situation and that spells "expensive" to their bargain-hunting mind.

Online it's more about what you don't say than what you do. If you don't use a menu header that reads "Locations" you aren't suggesting a chain, but instead a single store. Your "About Us" page should display a detailed bio that talks about the number of years you've been in business and that it was handed down from father to son (this is assuming you are the more exclusive store). You would feature a picture of your brick and mortar store in the header; your customers thereby realize that you are well-grounded and will be somewhere physical when the glass in the china hutch gets broken.

A more exclusive store has no need to feature badges of security from the Better Business Bureau or secured credit card handling. There are no "in-house financing with easy payment" plans. You may offer that a designer will visit their home rather than a "live chat" with someone overseas 24/7. Your brick and mortar hours are displayed and there is a telephone number rather than an email listed for contact.

A more exclusive store is likely to have a tasteful logo as it has graced a sign on the building for years. Building your site with these colors will extend that perception.

Enter the world of subliminal.

Chapter 5

The Subliminal World

This topic is so important to building a successful web presence that we will dedicate one entire chapter to it.

When was the last time you bought something unexpectedly and totally on impulse? Have you ever compared competing products and chosen one over the others for no obvious reason other than you "felt like it"? You have been overtaken by subliminal persuasion. You didn't even realize it. And that, my friend, was the whole idea.

The concept of subliminal persuasion is not all that new. It has actually been around as long as written communication. Interestingly enough, the earliest forms were not intended to be subliminal and their creators were unaware of their effect. Considered simply the artist's individual style, even with rough, charcoaled or carved pictographs on a cave wall, certain work was more admired than others. Their style suggested various emotions, including possibly aggression, perhaps an unusual weather event, a successful hunting season or recording new births in the tribal family. Therefore art in any form, is subliminally persuasive.

As a fledgling philosophy, subliminal persuasion found its infancy in the last century, but matured over the last four decades. Now it has advanced to the Internet and its immense communicative ability. How and why does it work and what are some examples? Let's look into its history for the answers.

So, what exactly is subliminal persuasion?

Persuasion is any external stimuli that when experienced creates a sensation of realization, awareness or need. In simpler terms, it makes you feel a reaction you may not ordinarily feel. The definition "subliminal" means that the stimulation takes place in the subconscious, to such an extent that the affected individual probably is not aware of it. Some say that it is similar to instinctive reaction, meaning that the experience triggers an inherited or genetically-based response.

It could be as simple as a ticking alarm clock that calms a puppy or kitten by mimicking the mother's heartbeat. Or, it might be as obvious as the color red, which when used in a coat of arms on a battlefield suggests warning and fear, blood and violence. Its power comes from the ability to manipulate the senses to achieve a particular reaction or suggestive stimulation.

Subliminal persuasion has a language of its own, and can be as powerful as a spoken word. It is often the result of one's own ancestral or societal environment and relies heavily on symbolism.

Its magic lies in its lack of conscious perception. Using the example of the red coat of arms; had their flag displayed the words, "We Will Kill You," the enemy would have been angered to react in a unified, defensive effort. Instead the simple color red suggested blood, dominance, aggression and warning. This made the enemy fearful, hesitant and less able to coordinate a unified response due to their individual reactions of fear. The color red suggests blood, and blood means injury and pain. It has been proven that when people stare at the color red for a long period of time, their blood pressure actually rises. When used in combination with a particular symbol, such as the logo of the American Red Cross, it suggests quite the opposite. This is, after all, a science.

Subliminal on the Internet

The Internet possesses immense communication potential. It is actually a television with hundreds of millions of channel selections where even the viewer can create their own experience. This level of persuasive power had to be recognized and there is no better utilization than that by Google and the other major search engines. In many cases, the advertisement and the content blend together so subtly that it is difficult to pick one apart from the other.

Take, for example, the personal blog. Think of them as a '70s talk show, either on radio or television. You have a host and they sponsor guests. The audience is the site visitor. The visitors are there because the topic is of interest to them. The Google advertising is the commercial.

But is that website really catering to your interest? Is it possible that you have been invited as a consumer, to buy and the content was the bait? Of course. So, why do you take part? Why do you visit the site even knowing that it's a commercial? It's because you gain something from the experience. It might be knowledge, it might be entertainment or perhaps you are socializing. What the site owner hopes is that you have come to be a customer. They are willing to create the beneficial experience; with the goal of keeping you long enough to buy their product. Perhaps the goal is not exactly a product, but to sign up for membership, to be added to a mailing list; whatever it is, you are expected to participate.

What makes you want to purchase? Is it gratitude to the site owner? No. This isn't an offering plate kind of experience. It is simply because you've had an emotional response to the experience and the product is something you now want to buy. You may genuinely have been looking for that product and this one looks so much better than its competition, or this may be a spur of the moment decision.

What has the site owner done to convert you to a customer? This may be entirely accidental on their part, but more likely there is some sort of subliminal message at work.

One of the most powerful aspects of subliminal messages is the way they can be interwoven into communication without the consumer being aware of it. Without subliminal, this would be a black and white world.

The Theory of Color

Science has learned that colors can generate specific responses. This is much more than having a 'favorite color.' It's an instinctive response.

Business has applied these expected responses to promote their products. They use them in branding; in their signs, product packaging, stationery, print advertising, websites, employee uniforms, transportation, buildings, interior design and more. The responses are so predictable that not only can business plant a brand in their customers' minds, but also they can actually 'hunt' for specific consumers.

Holiday Inn™, the expansive hotel chain operated for decades with their orange-lettered logo. Orange is a declassifying color and says "cheap." Holiday Inn™ built a customer base within family travelers, people who typically didn't have deep pockets, but often several children. As the destination fun parks built their own hotel complexes, Holiday Inn's™ customer base needed to expand. They decided to go after business travelers.

They had to re-design their 'look.' They converted their orange logo to dark green, a color that suggests success and money. To not abandon their family customers, they kept the orange in the asterisk dot of the "i" in "Holiday." Their conversion worked. Their percentage of business clients skyrocketed and they retained their family customers. All this was due to a change in a color.

Dark green is also commonly used in banks, insurance companies, jewelry stores and investment companies. Its suggestion of money, prosperity, safety and success makes their customers feel prosperous and secure. In the meantime, customers probably believed the dark green in the jewelry cases simply made the diamonds and gold stand out.

By contrast, airlines and hospitals do not use any shade of light green in their decors. That color suggests nausea. What color is your website?

More than RGB to Consider

Have you defined your ideal customer? Knowing who they are will help you in your subliminal messages.

What age group do they fall into? Are they wealthy, religious, female, business-oriented, active, do they love the outdoors? These are important first considerations.

Once you know your customer, what will they expect to find at your site? Entertainment? Education? Products for a hobby? Are they coming to your site to be convinced, looking for trust, to buy a service that requires efficiency? Define these profiles in order to know the proper tools to use.

Light, pastel colors appeal to an upscale audience. By contrast, primary colors (red, blue, green, bright yellow, purple, orange) appeal to children and older adults or those with minimal educations.

Men, who are very visual, like the darker colors. Red is an action color and has been determined to stimulate. It's a great color to use if your site is related to cars, sports, weight-loss or motivation. It can also cause your mouth to water. Perhaps this is due to eons of man hunting and killing animals for food? Aggression, anger, killing, blood, food?

Pink is a motivational color, with the added benefit of suggesting gentle loving, softness, relaxation and definitely female. It's a great color for health or personal improvement as it suggests change. Use caution, however, as a bright pink that is over-used can be promiscuous and cheap.

Blues are soothing, comfortable and heal the soul. Dark blue means justice, authority, wisdom and discipline. It is the color of business.

Browns are masculine colors, associated with the earth, woods, warmth and comfort. Brown is a passive color and is never worn by men who are in authority. Black, on the other hand, can be worn only by CEOs, presidents and funeral directors. That said, black can be used as an accent color and is certainly most effective in website text for legibility. It does suggest luxury and power, but when used with red, is ominous.

Yellows, the color of the sun, give people optimism and

joy; yellow cars are the least likely to be involved in accidents. It is a sociable color and soft, creamy yellows are very upper class. By contrast, dark or green-yellows suggest illness and is undesirable. Yellow does not sell and is only used safely with natural products such as corn or lemons.

Whites are pure, innocent, good, royal and wealthy. The use of white space with other strong colors can enhance both colors' qualities.

Colors which are opposite one another on a color wheel are complimentary colors, but that can mean they will not sit comfortably directly next to one another; an example are red and green. These holiday colors look nice when used in a mixture, but placing red type against a green background renders copy unreadable.

Knowing when and where to use colors can greatly affect your site.

Appearance and the Internet

Aside from the use of suggestive color, there are many means of using very effective persuasions to guide your website visitors toward your desired goal.

Assuming you have a product you wish to sell, the concept here is to identify your visitor and then create an environment that converts them into a customer. You must begin with a very clear understanding of your goal. If you don't understand it, your customer won't either.

The Landing Page

There is no more important location in Internet marketing. This is where you will direct the focus of advertising, press releases, word-of-mouth, backlinks and whatever other marketing tools you will employ. For this reason, the page must be very powerful. It is essentially a one-man sales force.

It's always a good idea to use split-testing methods to determine the finer responses to variations on the theme. With split-testing, you will create duplicates of your landing page, changing only one component, such as font, type-size or color, from one version to the next. Direct your web traffic to each of these variations in a balanced method and then use conventional traffic analyzers to determine which worked best to achieve your goal.

Is your page too busy? Remember that while many of your visitors may be on netbooks or laptops, still others are working with 24" or larger flat screens. That is a lot of visual square inch impact.

The top half of your landing page is the highest value real estate. It is what visitors will first see when they land on your site.

Use care when composing your copy. Some words will do the work for you; "**learn** from home", "**save** today", "**discover** what the competition is doing." These are movement words and people are trained to act in response. You will have about six seconds to grab your visitor's attention and keep them engaged so be sure this area of your site is a direct reflection of what the visitor expects to find. If they are visiting via a Google ad or other pay-per-click campaign, they expect to see the keywords they used prominently displayed within that six second's worth of reading.

Keep your landing page clean of interfering messages. Use a single call to action that discourages them clicking away to another page. For example, if your product bears further explanation or you want to give the visitor general information, such as an FAQ, expanded contact info, general industry facts, etc., move these to secondary pages and connect them using text links. The search engines will spider those and present them as individual pages, but you won't draw attention to them and lose your visitor as you're moving them to the point of action.

Just as a good story has a beginning, middle and end, the landing page must tell the full story. The end, of course, is where you motivate them to commit to whatever you are "selling." We have all heard stories since we were small children and the copy you present should be well-written and free of spelling and punctuation errors. Use a "voice" that your visitor will identify with. Only use graphics that augment your persuasive argument, not just as random decoration. Graphics can slow down page loading and that itself, is a negative subliminal message. Whatever images you choose to use, be sure they are high quality. Using free clip art imparts "start-up" and "suspicious" to your visitor and you will lose them. If you don't have the software or graphic skills to produce top-flight art, hire someone to do it for you.

Avoid These

The following are considered interruptive and as such, should be avoided. You want your visitor to be fully engaged and not frustrated or they will click away.

- Flashing ads and banners
- Pop-ups
- Excessive video for decoration's purpose
- Automatic music
- Misspelled words
- Neon
- Poor quality or too plentiful graphics
- Personal tastes of the web designer – concentrate on

the visitor's expectation

- Too many ads, no matter how much money they represent
- Too little white space – the eye needs a rest
- Single-column, full-width sentences
- Links that lead no where, or worse yet, to another page in the site without navigation
- Using the competition's logo in any way – you've just given them a brand impression
- Sleazy tricks like windows that will not close

Speaking the Language

Learn the language of your ideal visitor. If the focus of your site is a topic you aren't particularly familiar with, learn it. Visitors want to feel lulled into a trustful mood by the presence of "work-speak" – those phrases, attitudes, euphemisms and acronyms common to their area of interest.

As an illustration, if your site is meant to attract NASCAR fans, you will want to dial in the language of the racing industry. Using high-tech language will point out your novice standing and the trust level from your visitor will be non-existent.

Or let's say your site is made for literary types; for librarians, teachers and those who love Shakespeare. Are you someone who cannot remember the difference between fiction and non-fiction? Would you make the mistake of referring to a book as a non-fictional novel? This may seem silly, but if you consider that one of the top-grossing products sold through the Internet is books, you can see this is serious business.

The old expression in the literary world of "write what you know" holds true on the Internet as well. Again, if you're not familiar with your topic or your writing skills are short of the mark, don't cut corners here. Find someone to help you who knows what they're doing.

Chapter 6

Perspective

Everything, absolutely everything in life, is a matter of perspective. To the man who is starving, a found dollar is a cup of hot soup; to the man who has millions, it's not worth bending to pick up.

There is a successful television show named Undercover Boss whose story line from week to week features the owner/CEO of a company donning a disguise and working elbow to elbow with ground level employees in his or her company. The show depicts the boss discovering the "little" people who have made his company great and their ideas or problems that otherwise go unrecognized by upper management.

Have you lost touch with your employees, or more importantly perhaps, your customers?

Fredrik Meijer, founder of the Midwest super store chain bearing his last name, discovered that truth. His stores (which pre-dated Walmart in the concept of combining groceries on one side and department store wares on the other) were built with similar floor plans that were designed to put the more profitable products nearest the door. The pharmacy, for one, was always located at the back of the store. Meijer began to deal with illness as he aged and upon entering one of his stores to have a prescription filled, realized that people who were sick and aged were doing two things: 1) they were not buying other merchandise, they simply wanted the best price on prescriptions and to go home and 2) these ailing customers had to walk the entire depth of his monster stores to get to the pharmacy. His solution was to move the pharmacy up to the front of his stores, just inside the door that lead to non-grocery aisles. At many of his stores he added a drive-through window.

Have you tried your customers' perspective? Have you structured your business so that the highest profit products and services are easily accessible while the possibly lower profit, but more often sought after, are more difficult to find? How does this truly affect your bottom line? Do you lose sales simply because the effort for the customer is too great and they go elsewhere? Why do you suppose that in small town America, the two businesses that continue to thrive are the corner grocery and the hardware store? If you need just one screw, are you going to traipse ¼ mile through Walmart to buy an entire package and then wait in the checkout line for 15 minutes, only to discover that you bought the wrong size because there was no one in the hardware department to help you?

Become your own customer. What is your business known for and how did it gain recognition among your customers? Are you known for low prices? Highest quality? Customer service? Multiple locations? Hard to find products? Huge inventory?

Taking the latter, inventory, how can you replicate that consumer expectation in an online sense? How can you set yourself apart from your competition?

Ask book selling behemoth Amazon. Just ten years ago, almost any small town had a local bookseller and larger metro areas, including malls and airports, were peppered with Waltons, Barnes & Noble and Borders chains. You looked to your local small store to remember what you liked to read and to order new titles in, particularly with you, in mind. The larger chain stores boasted inventory and selection—thus if you were looking for a book mentioned at last Saturday's dinner party, it was a pretty good bet Barnes & Noble had it on the shelf.

But what happened when they didn't? After all, there was a limit to their bookshelf space and once a title went off the bestseller list, it was probably replaced by one that was still ranked. Sure, they could order it in for you, but the inventory would come from publisher's stock and that could take a couple of weeks or more—assuming it was even still in print. Enter Amazon and the digital publishing era.

Amazon prided itself on carrying every book and shipping it within 24 hours. Titles that were backlisted (no longer in print) were entered into the digital print catalogs and that copy of 1984 could be printed off and shipped from the Amazon dock in 72 hours or less. Exit Barnes & Noble. Lock the door your local bookseller.

The result was that Jeff Bezos, CEO of Amazon, just purchased The Washington Post for $250 million; a complete shift in fortunes and power. Amazon's print and audio book divisions were buyouts of other successful companies. This from a man who started his company in his garage and after inviting 300 friends to test out his website, he began selling books within 30 days to the US and 45 foreign countries. Bezos and his 300 friends were his customers and that first-hand perspective permitted him to build a machine that crippled an entire, time-honored industry.

Amazon's explosion was due, only in part, to books. They began to acquire other products—which were housed in their online "departments." Just as a large building has several entrances, customers enter a site online through the portal offered up by a search engine. Google "books" and Amazon comes up. Google "toys" and Amazon comes up. Google "electronics" and Amazon comes up. You can even Google "baby clothes" and Amazon comes up. Not on page four of results, but on page one.

Look at your own business and ask yourself, "If shelf space or storage were not an issue, what sort of products/services would I add?" You don't need to have everything in the back room in order to offer it to your customers.

Using the earlier example, when you Google "baby clothes" you'll find Amazon comes in at the top of the search results – before industry giants Kohl's, Carter's, The Gap and Babies R Us. And you thought they only sold books?

Interestingly, when you shop the Amazon baby clothes, you'll find the well-known brand Ralph Lauren. If you order one of these tiny designer cuties, you'll see that Amazon only fulfills the order; they don't offer it directly.

This brings to your option table the concept of affiliation. How many products/services can you think of that would serve your existing customer base and raise your bottom line—if only you had them on hand in your store? A virtual store has unlimited shelf space and you need not even warehouse the products. An affiliation with the manufacturer or distributor gives you the product on your virtual shelf and a computer key click triggers the shipment directly from your affiliated business to your customer – with your label on the box.

Think of this as adding potentially thousands of departments to your store/company and offering a branded entrance to each of these without requiring the customer to "walk to the back of your store" to find them. How many items can you stick up front by the door?

When Amazon wanted to improve on its shipping time, it located its shipping warehouse across the street from the world's largest book distributor. When that wasn't fast enough, it just went out and bought an ailing digital printing company—the precursor to the Kindle concept of ebooks.

Fix It

Another advantage to taking your business online is that it forces you to analyze how you've done business in the offline world. Any good manager can sit down with a pad of paper and write down ten things that could be improved in the way he does business. Try it.

Could you offer more staff to help customers? Could you offer a larger inventory so that customer who is craving instant gratification won't leave you and go down the street? Would your customers buy more if you offered financing? How much more could you sell if the man in the brown uniform dropped it off at their door in 24 hours?

Just consider, for example, how many people literally cannot climb into a car or bus and get to you? Perhaps they're too old to drive or live where they can't have a car? Perhaps they can't even afford a car. Does that mean they wouldn't be a good customer for you? Did you realize that according to the U.S. Census Bureau, more than 20% of the U.S. population is disabled in some sense and may not even be able to get to your store? Let's add to that the 35 million Americans who are over the age of 65 and it doesn't take long to see the birth of a mammoth customer base that you probably currently can't touch. That said, the Census Bureau also reports that more than 75% of the households in the US have access to a computer. That figure was in 2011, so it has greatly grown since then.

In summary, you are able to not only add unlimited

square footage to your store and warehouse, you can now serve an additional 97 million American customers. Shall we walk a bit south and north and include Mexico and Canada? How about the rest of the world? Now you can see why Jeff Bezos started in his garage in 1994 and now is one of the richest and most powerful men on the planet; a lonely little bookseller. He wasn't even big enough to have his own store on the corner – think about it!

What other things could you fix in your company? Could your cash flow be improved if every customer paid in advance? Could you serve more customers if you were open 24/7 and had unlimited salespeople to help?

What if the customers learned to help themselves?

Imagine if you never had to take time to answer the telephone? Now the bothersome teenager who asks, "Do you have these in size 6 in pink?" doesn't waste your time. Instead, you point her to the drop downs on the web page and say, "What we have is listed right there."

Picture your entire sales process now, and how it would change in an online scenario.

"Hello? Thompson Mercantile, may I help you?"

"Uh, yeah, uh...do you guys sell widgets?"

"What brand of widget, sir?"

"Uh, I don't know. My lawnmower quit running and when I took it apart, this part was smashed. Probably was the kid knocking his bike against it every time he throws it in the shed, you know? You have any kids?"

"Yes, sir. What brand is your lawnmower?"

"Uh, not sure. The wife bought it at a yard sale four years ago and the name was all scratched off. It's red

and weighs at least 200 lbs."

"Well, sir, we probably wouldn't have the part you needed. We only carry inventory for parts on mowers up to three years old."

"Well, that's silly. A good lawnmower won't even break by three years – so what good is it to have parts for a mower that ain't been broke yet?"

"Well, sir, we just don't have room to carry every part for every mower ever since they've been made."

"Huh. Well, do you think one of the newer parts would work on my older mower?"

"Sir, I'm afraid I wouldn't know."

"Should I bring it down and have you take a look at it?"

"Well, sir, you could, but we charge a $25 estimate fee."

"$25??? Just to look at a mower? Not even fix it? Well, that's just plain immoral. You're never gonna sell new mowers to folks who you charge $25 to look at their broke ones."

"Yes, sir. Perhaps it's time for a new mower?"

"Nah, can't afford a new one. How much are your new mowers?"

"They start at $400 and go up to $5,000 for the heavy duty riding mowers with attachments."

"$5,000 for a dang lawn mower? For that kind of money I could hire somebody to mow my yard. It ain't very big. I can mow it in about 10 minutes…when my mower's workin'."

"Is there anything else I can help you with, sir? We're open until 8:00 pm this evening if you'd like to come in and look. We have some nice used models that would be very affordable."

"Nah, I'll just borrow the neighbor's." Click.

While that may sound exaggerated, chances are you can remember a comparable conversation. In an online environment, the customer does the work. They look up their own part numbers or buy a new unit without asking you time-wasting questions. You become, what the sales world has long termed, "an order-taker." While that designation was cause for embarrassment in the halls of great salesmen, ask Jeff Bezos whether he'd rather be rich, or be answering the phone.

Chapter 7

Adding the Numbers

One of the greatest aspects of doing business on the Internet is the amount of data that's available.

Imagine right now that you are the Mercantile used in the conversation example of the last chapter. If you're in a medium-sized town, you probably have at least a half dozen competitors. What do you know about their businesses? You might meet the owners at the Rotary luncheon, but everyone puts on their best face and wants to be envied. The guy from the hardware store down the street isn't going to tell you his customer traffic is down and he hasn't sold a single artificial Christmas tree even though his wife spent the whole weekend decorating his front window with them. He won't want to let on that he's not as popular as the big name store at the edge of town or that he's selling widgets for a dollar more each and suspects that might be why. In fact, he's going to tell you as little about his business as possible, and there's no point of your going into his store to spy; everyone in town knows you.

You've probably been running your business for years

without knowing much at all about the competition, and very likely not enough about your own business.

Do you know how much your average customer spends?

Do you know where each of your customers lives?

How about what brought them into your store?

Did they leave with a good or lousy experience and are they likely to recommend others?

If you stayed open longer on Saturdays, would it be worth it?

How do you compare to the guy down the street or the chain store at the edge of town?

Would these numbers help you? Of course they would!

Let's check over at your online store now. Ask yourself the same questions.

Do you know how much your average customer spends?

Absolutely. The database maintains these figures and you're able to filter results to show you not only how much they spent, but what they bought, whether they've bought from you before, and more importantly, you now know what they're likely to buy in the future. If they bought a lawn mower, it's a good idea to show them your weed eaters and garden tools while they're in the lawn maintenance mood. In fact, you can offer an upsell at checkout and perhaps substantially increase the amount of the sale.

Do you know where each of your customers lives? Well, unless you delivered the goods, probably not. Online, however, you will know their name, their address, their phone, their credit card number and their email address. You can send them offers when the weed eaters go on sale or snow shovels when the Fall rolls around.

How about what brought them into your store? Unless they mention specifically, you won't know whether they were recommended by a friend, attracted by your front window display, saw your ad in the local paper or your listing in the Yellow Pages. You won't know what works and what is a waste of money. Online, however, you can track when they came to your store, where they were referred from and where they went when they left you. How? Magic. No, actually, it's Google Analytics and it's free. What can you do with that information? I'll bet you can figure it out.

Did they leave with a good or lousy experience and are they likely to recommend others? The last place you want to hear this is from the Better Business Bureau or overhear it from the next aisle at the grocery. Online, however, your customer can "Like" you on Facebook, will likely respond to an incentive-based survey, and you may even find yourself gracing a page at angieslist.com. But better yet, you can, with an affiliate program, get all sorts of people, including total strangers, to host your products on their own websites. This commission-based reference spreads the word for you and the result is your business grows and you only pay sales reps for what they actually sell.

If you stayed open longer on Saturdays, would it be worth it? What does three hours more on Saturday cost you? Salaries, utilities, goodwill at home? What does it cost you online? $0. Heck, at that rate, you can afford to be open 24/7/365. You won't even need keys to your front door and you can leave the lights on forever because your customer is paying for the electricity.

How do you compare to the guy down the street or the chain store at the edge of town? Now this is where the Internet really shines. Again, if we visit Google we can ascertain who is more popular, including why. We can check Alexa and see how you, as well as your competition, compares to the rest of the world. You can visit the competition, day or night, and try out their customer's experience, see their pricing, ask questions of their customer service staff, check out what's on sale, compare business models and even leave a few snide comments on their customer feedback if you like. For that matter, you can buy product from them and re-sell it as an affiliate, thereby riding their coat tails. What's not to like about that? In the meantime, Google Analytics will give you so much information about who your customer is, where they came from, how long they stayed on your site, where they entered and where they left, who referred them, what they looked at, whether they came from an ad and actually WHICH ad – you will hardly know what to do with all that information. But you will soon figure out that it will allow you to position yourself so precisely that you can almost predict every dollar you'll make over the upcoming year.

That sort of knowledge is invaluable. Are more people buying widgets A or B? Why? If it's widget A, get rid of widget B, but then, heck, it's not costing you anything to carry it so keep it around—it's not taking up any room.

Break down the numbers. Want to increase your sales by 25% over the next year? Let's walk the path. You know:

1. where the customer is coming from so you can increase your visibility there, whether it's advertising you're paying for, membership in an organization, word of mouth from a manufacturer, etc.

2. how much the customer is spending on average, and whether more products, faster delivery, lower prices, better sales or customer service are making the difference

3. when the customer is most likely to shop your site; if it's after midnight then offer a midnight-6 am customer appreciation sale so you eliminate the competition entirely

4. how long the customer is staying on your site and where they're exiting tells you which areas need to be improved; how long does it take to change the store? As long as it takes for your web person to type it and hit "upload"

5. your overhead – which can be advertising, wages, hosting fees, merchant card percentage – all the numbers are there.

So, if you want to double your business, you know precisely what to do to make that happen. It may be increasing your traffic, it may be directing your advertising at a different demographic, it might include offering more products, perhaps a store or branding re-design; all these factors can now be fairly gauged and your plan implemented.

Do you see what has happened? You are completely in control. Growing your business is no more complicated than adjusting dials that are clearly marked and have an expected outcome. When you ask yourself, "Will this work?" you have hard statistical data that takes the gamble out of the question. Adjusting and fine-tuning can take place in a matter of minutes. No bigger parking lots or more elevators are needed; your building is unlimited and you configure it exactly as wanted using the magic wand of a keyboard and mouse.

Need more help? Find a freelancer or engage a company with a call center; it's that simple. That said, you will find that the more self-serving your customer can be, the more he or she will buy. It is common for the salesperson to actually get in the way of impulse buying. The customer can be put on the defensive; fearing judgement or the inspection of credit worthiness. The psychology of buying online means you use plastic and can do it without leaving any other trail. Wives can order a new wardrobe at 3 a.m. while hubby is snoring. Husbands can order that new hunting rifle while the wife is at the grocery store. No trips to the store, no justification for the purchase, no "well, you bought that so I get to buy this." It's clean, pure, fun consumerism.

Consider for just a moment the simplification of your bookkeeping. Everything is paid for in advance, so there are no statements to send out and no collections to be endured. You don't have to verify whether a check is good; the card processor does that all for you automatically. The money is simply deposited into your bank account and all the numbers, names and addresses come with it. You can use a processor such as PayPal and deal with customers from all over the world in their native currencies.

At the same time, it's important to look at savings as an improvement in your bottom line as well. Your online store has very little cost of doing business, unless it's in shipping orders. There are no sales reps with fleets of company cars and expense accounts. You don't have to add 100,000 square feet in office space and fill it with desks, computers, human resources and company insurance plans. The customer helps himself and almost all of the rest of it is automated. Your liability is hugely diminished and when it's time to update the company stationery and business forms, you click a new color in Photoshop and it's done.

You no longer spend thousands or tens of thousands on shotgun approach advertising, hoping for a 2% return in sales. Instead you can see the metrics for how each ad performs and adjust or cancel it in seconds. In many cases your advertising will be seen by millions and you will only pay a pre-set amount per person who actually enters your store. Once they're there, it's up to you to keep them.

Essentially, you have ultimate control and nowhere to go but up in sales. That's about as close to a guarantee as anyone can come in the business world.

CHAPTER 8

What's on the Shelf?

In any store down the street, you'll find products on shelves, displays or other creative presentations. Services are generally listed on some sort of menu and are accompanied by pricing.

When it comes time to change pricing, out comes the pricing gun and new stickers must replace those you will peel off. If things are on a menu, new menus must be designed. This tends to discourage day-by-day supply and demand; something which governs your bottom line.

In your online store, you have the ability to change pricing with a single key click – and any time you wish. You can also create special offers or coupons on demand. With an established mailing list you can track your buyers' spending and offer them custom-tailored offers that will appeal to their personal desires.

This provides an almost undeniable opportunity for buyers to purchase from you. With a bit of creative programming you can create offers that cannot be surpassed. Assuming you have done your research and are serving a dedicated niche, buying from you simply becomes a matter of time.

Right about now, if you're not already implementing these opportunities, you're probably anxious to get started. Each day that you put this decision off can be likened to trying to feed and care for yourself in an endless room full of pitfalls in total darkness. Each move becomes a gamble.

A tactically designed website, however, can be so finely tuned as to remove the risk. Buying habits can be anticipated and addressed before the customer even realizes they want to buy.

What Do I Sell?

You may be looking at your shelves and wondering whether everything you carry can be sold on the Net. The answer is, yes, and more…

Originally, the Internet was the store for products and services unique to itself. Domain buying/selling, website building and advertising were the coins of trade. The fact that people acquired computers and through the use of search engines were kind enough to separate themselves into neat little niches, could not be ignored for long. Enterprising individuals soon began to target these niches and use the readily accessed demographics to sell products and services.

As commerce shifted more and more from Main Street to dot.com Street, companies were literally forced to adapt or fail. One huge example is the media; Twitter almost single-handedly decapitated an industry that was hundreds of years old.

There is no question that the Internet has impacted business as a laboratory of innovation. Prior to the Internet there was no widespread need to accept foreign currencies at your business. However, once you begin doing business with customers across the planet, that need exploded in demand.

Elon Musk was one such entrepreneur who answered the call; building through mergers the empire of PayPal. PayPal has since been purchased by eBay for $1.5 billion in stock and Elon has gone on to explore his dreams of clean energy and space. He is currently testing a rocket that can launch space vehicles safely and then return to Earth, refuel and be ready to fire again within days. This steps into the fundamental industries of trucking, railroads and aeronautics; something that would not have been attempted by anyone who wasn't already embedded in these fields. In short, the re-useable rocket has come about due to harnessing the immense opportunities on the Internet.

If you stand back and look at this, you have to recognize that the way you currently conduct offline business is more than likely beginning to decline. It simply cannot stand up to the possibilities that a global audience will demand. Therefore, you have to begin to look at what you're doing and plan for not a year ahead, but a decade ahead. This is much more easily accomplished if you have already harnessed the demographics available through an online presence.

What role does your company play in that future? Are you a creator of content? Will your input be involved in establishing trends? Do you sell tangible products? Will you harness an international workforce to increase profits and gradually balance the commercialism the U.S. currently enjoys with the billions of potential consumers offered from countries such as China? Will you, such as Elon Musk, be availed an opportunity that could not exist offline? This is up to you.

Let's look at some potential conversions of offline products and services to an online, global market.

The first one you have to acknowledge is publishing. This was a particularly easy target simply because the process was conducted behind heavy, ancient doors and newcomers were seldom invited inside. Fortunately, the consumers, people who bought books, like you and I, did not care where the content originated. They were simply hungry for more. Lo and behold, there were people quite capable of providing that content who did not hold publishing contracts!

Thus, the advent of digital publishing lowered the threshold of publishing a book to something even a kid could handle; in some cases, there was no cost. Thus, more and more writers jumped into the fracas and while marketing still is the hurdle they need to accomplish, the content is, indeed there.

You can literally write a book in a week or less and have it available to a global audience a day later. Need to change paragraph four on page 100? No problem. Reword it, upload it and it's changed. Want it printed on paper? No problem. It ships tomorrow. Have a customer in the UK? No problem; we have a printing plant there, too. You upload your file to one server and plants all over the world can access it and print it. Your royalty comes into your PayPal or mailbox at the end of the month. This did not exist 20 years ago; it is a new technology that replaced an old, and the world has benefitted.

Let's look at shoes. Now, the customer who happened to have very wide feet was often forced to settle for orthopedic shoes that could be purchased locally; unless they happened to fly to New York City every time they needed new leather. Today, however, companies such as Zappos offers a huge selection of shoes, in every conceivable size and width. That customer no longer settles; they now order attractive footwear, can have it delivered the next morning, try it on in the comfort of their home and if it doesn't fit—drop it off at the nearest UPS outlet and let them take care of it. No cost for shipping returns and your credit card is refunded in days. Zappos seized upon a concept that limited shoe sellers everywhere and by coordinating supply with demand, re-generated an industry.

Need a lawyer? Can't afford one? Today you can hop over to LegalZoom and purchase a valid will for each of the 50 states. An attorney, familiar with your state's particular laws will answer questions, one at a time, for $35. Want to incorporate? $300. Want to become a landlord? $99. The law can be bought, and companies such as LegalZoom made it affordable for everyone. Again, a rather untouchable industry for the common man, coordinated for the average consumer.

Just consider some of the services you can have performed today via the Internet:

- a college degree
- having your horoscope read
- choosing a hairstyle or personalized wardrobe design
- simple medical care and access to having online radiologists to read your scan or x-ray
- private detective
- gambling
- food delivery
- video telephone across the planet
- movies, music and other arts and entertainments
- home schooling
- a yard sale
- matchmaking
- marriage
- binding legal contracts
- home purchasing

The list goes on and on. You might wonder how your particular industry can be adapted to the Internet. The thing to remember is that this will not be determined by what you have to offer as much as what consumers want to buy. Convenience is the number one factor and affordability the second; this trumps branding and fad by far.

Under that sort of vision, take a tangible product such as the lonely chocolate chip cookie you bake in your basement kitchen. It has a shelf life of maybe one day before it's garbage. That limits your customers to those within driving distance. However, get an audience for that cookie and using the power of the Internet, attract global orders and have the man from FedEx deliver it anywhere in the world by tomorrow morning. Once you have an audience, you can contract with people everywhere to reproduce your recipe as a satellite baking location. You've now doubled your reach in days and increased your customer base and affordability exponentially. How difficult would it have been to organize such a business prior to the Internet?

So, sit back in your chair and instead of trying to re-create what you're already doing in an online environment— re-create your concept of the possibilities. If you combined a global customer base with the logistics and organization the Internet offers; how could you evolve your business and therefore become the company your competitors envy? Re-invent yourself and your business.

CHAPTER 9

Selling Information

This is not a chapter about current headlines, but about the value of information and how it is transacted on the Internet.

When people first began to discover the Net, they were excited to have a platform where they could show off a bit. The very spirit of the Internet was in sharing; indeed that is how it began. People were quick to jump aboard and share everything they knew. From recipes for fruitcake to how-to's for fixing your clothes dryer, the information was there. Search engines evolved to handle this dearth of content, and as they did so, the concept of selling information began.

You may be surprised what people are willing to pay to find out. You may be even more surprised at what information is readily available for simple sharing.

Is information a product you have to offer? What sort of personal or professional experience has value to others? This changes all the time. Twenty years ago few people cared how to build a website; in fact many resented the introduction of acme.com's website listing in their television advertising. The word, "Internet" was spat out by angry consumers who equated it with downtown peep shows and graffiti. True, some of the baser desires of consumers popped up there first; generally because it was a lawless arena to reach a great many people.

That has all changed. Now, knowing how to not only build a website, but one that is highly functional and refined in a way that ensures it makes money, is invaluable. The professional CEOs of two decades ago now are young people with keyboards.

Take a look, for example, at the real estate market. An agent's worst nightmare is the client who wants to see a hundred houses and then decides not to move after all. How much gas, time and patience does that cost the agent? How many sales did they miss while dealing with this one potential client?

So agents moved online. It was a natural selection. They had photos, information and were waiting to tap into a larger audience than people who happened to drive by one of their for sale signs. A laptop and a cell phone gave them portable offices in their cars.

This birthed a new generation in their industry. Suddenly anyone who was interested in buying a foreclosure hungered for information about how to do it. People who were planning to re-locate across country could narrow down their search ahead of time via the Net. They could compare properties, check on current property taxes, Google Earth view the area and what it had to offer, research the schools, churches and medical care the area provided. They could apply for mortgage pre-qualification and price insurance and moving costs. They could sign up for cable television and have their telephone transferred. There was, in fact, very little need for the customer to visit an area before actually buying the house.

They became highly educated buyers. The work of an

agent was greatly reduced, but their necessity was shifted to a source of information. The progressive agent built a reputation for knowing which foreclosures were good buys and which were nightmares about to happen. They knew where businesses were likely to expand and where they were to close. They had access to property information that had yet to be entered into computers. They could explain the logic of investing in multi-family dwellings. They understood the deals for first time homebuyers and how you qualify for special financing in blighted areas.

They had the information. More importantly, their efforts in learning all this paid off many times more because they weren't helping just a small handful of potential customers; they were addressing a much larger audience and could actually control where someone moved based on the opportunities in living there.

They sold it. Sometimes in a book, or simply through their website. They taught seminars in real estate investment through membership sites they built and offered expert opinions on concepts that most homebuyers had never considered. Designers jumped in to provide 3-D, 360-degree home viewings online and insurance agents began developing Twitter followers. It was an industry revolution and those who knew what they were doing offered to sell what they knew—for a price.

Yes, if your life's goal is to find out how KFC makes their fried chicken, you can find it on the Net. But if you want to leverage what you know to people who want to learn it—you are sitting on a goldmine.

Chapter 10

Who Will Wear the Hats?

As you look around in your current business, most likely you have employees who each command a certain area of responsibility. Perhaps it's just you, in which case you carry all the weight of sales, production, fulfillment, bookkeeping and inventory control. You may be at the point where you're just about ready to expand enough that you will need more employees.

Regardless of where you stand, it's likely you feel that you, as well as anyone who works for you, is just about at the limit of what they can handle. It is a human trait to practice Parkinson's law, which essentially says that no matter how small your workload, you will instinctively expand it to fill the allotted time. This is most likely an instinct of preservation.

The result, however, is that as a manager, it's difficult to be objective about just how busy everyone is. When it comes to starting a small business, the two primary points of failure are undercapitalization and the lack of planned expansion.

Undercapitalization

To contemplate expansion in an offline situation, as we've discussed earlier, you are looking at physical commitments to structure and personnel—and very likely inventory and other infrastructure as well. This entails considerable planning and naturally, investment of capital. Very often this involves raising funds through personal contribution, investors or outright loans from banks.

In building a business, one looks to the future and often the goal is expansion. Many companies need time to adjust to the practicalities of a whole scale expansion and this can affect the ongoing business on a day-to-day level.

Then there's the debt, which is by nature leveraged over the future, whether it is short term or long makes no difference. It is an additional expense an existing business entity must take on during a time when expansion creaks are already placing a stress.

Then there are the external factors such as the economy, acts of God and the competition getting the jump on you and capturing part of your projected future market. The result is if this process is not timed perfectly, it can mean the end of the business as a whole.

Poorly Planned Expansion

In an online situation, much of the expansion risk is eliminated and the transition is far smoother. Again, we refer to the endless real estate of a website and the fact that adding a service is often no more than an automated process your web designer includes. You can repurpose hidden commodities that may not be evident in an offline environment, but become not only apparent, but in demand online.

An example could be a business that sells gift baskets. In the physical world, the customer will want to see and touch the products to be included in the basket, if only to ensure that quality is consistent. The business owner may not be able to offer as much selection do to storage limitations or the fact that food included in the basket can only remain fresh for a limited period. To manage these variables, the business owner is forced to pre-select an assortment of basket contents, limiting what they have to offer.

Online, that business offers a broader selection and the quality factor is expected. Customers select according to a picture and it is the responsibility of the business to ensure the actual item lives up to the expectation. Food is purchased according to the order (which has been pre-paid). This means they're able to buy bread fresh from the bakery for shipping and not maintain a dozen loafs on the shelf "just in case." Consequently, their hidden commodity becomes the ability to let the customer "mix and match" basket contents according to their own preferences and budgets. There is no waste and the customer enjoys total freedom.

Now the business owner can expand their business to online real estate and there are no additions of personnel, real estate, office infrastructure or investment capital. In fact, if anything the online version of the company has a "rubber band" expansion capability in that its size is dictated by the customers' needs and purchases, rather than in pre-establishing an offering of goods and services.

When it comes to transition, the website costs no more to run at one size than another. Think of this as a business with an elastic waistband…if the extra inches are needed, they're ready to go to work. If not, they retract until needed and the transition is gradual enough the customers do not notice.

The Fulfillment Aspect

"But..." you interrupt. "Who is going to fill all those new orders?" This is a problem every business owner dreams about. This is where good planning comes into play.

Look at the requirements of fulfillment objectively. What is needed foremost and how will your existing logistics change?

Do you need to increase inventory? Depending on what you offer, most likely you can come up with a "just in time" approach that allows you to keep your investment capital in the bank. You will leverage cash from new orders to make the purchases and on a very large scale, the mere possession of interest-bearing funds can raise your bottom line. Ask the folks who invest in the foreign exchange about that. Even if you do need to have more inventory on hand, you can capture profit from buying in bulk and remember—the orders guarantee your cash flow.

Will you need to hire more employees? In the miracle that comes with proper website design, your customers become your employees. They type in their relevant information, choose what they want, pay for it at the checkout and track the delivery all by themselves.

What about needing more capital? Why would you? Actual sales force that elastic waistband to stretch outward. You are free to shop for more ideal suppliers and to add their products to your line at will. Who could ask for more than that?

So, perhaps the only people you will need are those who count the money? Not true. Computers do that automatically and the funds are tracked and deposited in your bank account. A simple CSV export and your existing account just puts in the new numbers.

The Digital Factor

One trend businesses are discovering is the asset of digital products. What sort of knowledge do you have that might be marketable? Have you considered writing a book and establishing yourself as an expert? Would you like to sponsor other experts in your field as an endorsement? Perhaps host an online seminar that benefits your customer. Include valuable information, tables, calculators and reference materials into your site. Become the authority site for your entire field.

Look at the competition and at other companies whose model would also work for you. You will find all sorts of examples of how digital products can become yet another thing you have to offer to your customer.

Chapter 11

Outsourcing:
The Workforce that Never Stops

Even if you are a lone entrepreneur, working by a single light bulb in your basement, you have need of growth. If nothing more than to duplicate your own efforts, you will, at some point, need to call in the services of others as you expand online. It's more likely, however, that you'll want to utilize skills you don't already possess.

This is an expensive proposition. Full-time, dedicated employees bring with them the need to make payroll, obtain health insurance coverage, secure competitive benefits to offer and immerse you in governmental paperwork.

If you are a larger company and adding an employee may be not a problem, you still have to look at the same issues when you need only certain expertise on a limited basis. For example, let's say you need someone to illustrate your product line for inclusion on your site? How much will one competent artist with all these skills cost you and what do you do with them once the site is complete? Answer email? That's a bit of a waste.

Using freelance professionals, supervised by a highly competent consultant, frees you up to do what you do best. It allows you to retain the personal brand you have brought to your customers, while augmenting what you have to offer. Freelancers are to business what mocha lattés are to a cup of coffee, but at the same cost.

This sort of "rubber-band" staff allows you to meet any level of demand without incurring the cost of training, salary and benefits, office space, tax obligations and the distasteful burden of letting people go if the workload drops off. Freelancers *expect* to be temporary, so you get their best performance for the entire project.

Business owners considering expanding online can be concerned about the new skill sets needed to make the site successful.

Business requires flexibility and responsiveness. That's where the big corporate structures fail; they just can't turn on a dime when the opportunity calls for it. You, however, can do just that.

With a managing consultant, hiring freelance workers enables you to:

- Offer 24/7 telephone support for customers in every time zone

- Modify staffing to handle unexpected highs and lows in sales

- Offer your customers professional expertise without economic commitment

- Utilize high-end, rapidly obsolete computer software and equipment without investment or expensive staff training

- Tap into massive marketing power

- Review recommendations before hiring

- Move quickly, literally within hours, to develop any aspect of business including general staffing, concept, sales, marketing, IT, customer service and more

- Enhance your company's profile and consumer offerings without encumbering overhead

- Give your "small" business that unique "big" business profile

Using a talented, willing, inexpensive, readily available, professionally-equipped staff to augment your already successful business position simply makes sense. Using staffing resources around the world, makes even more sense. It is important, however, that you have a trusted consultant in place to manage not only the components needed for your business, but ensures compatibility and the time frame in which these are implemented.

CHAPTER 12

Good Will Hunting

As a company, customer goodwill is critically important. No customer-company relationship is going to be perfect. If you're in business you will recognize that one rotten apple client from a mile off, but you're not always in a position to refuse to serve them. That's where goodwill comes in.

Even when the relationship is not a perfect match, a good and positive overall customer experience can often patch over the rough spots. This can be particularly helpful in an online environment where you are likely never to see your customers face to face. That depersonalization is always a bit of an adjustment for any company whose sales staff is used to shaking hands and looking a customer in the eye as they assess their needs and response.

There are, however, a number of ways you can accomplish this in the virtual environment. Here are some options to consider.

The first thing you will want to do is to check out your

online competition. This is who your customer will also see and you want to look good by comparison. Gauge what they're offering and either match or improve upon it—that's the behavior that can put you ahead.

This is particularly true if you're David battling Goliath. Large corporate entities who have moved online, struggle with developing a one-on-one relationship with customers, simply because they're not used to doing that. They are generally shielded behind distributors, partnerships or rules that isolate them from the consumer response.

The next thing to do is to look at your existing customer interaction. Do you have sales reps as a necessary component to each transaction? Do you go out personally and handle every deal? Do you have a suggestions box on the front counter? What about your return policy? How often do you offer sales? Are your current hours matching your customers' needs?

A good goal is to not only meet/adapt your customer service, but to improve upon it. Remember that no matter how anonymous the Internet may seem, each customer is in the middle of a personal consumer experience when they visit your site, and Google ensures the world will remember it forever.

Do you offer a reminder service that tells your customer they're about due for a refill/renewal/warranty policy? Online this is an automated process and you can make the language as personal as you like; substituting their first and last name, their city or even comments like, "I see it's raining in your area today...". The nice part is that the customer feels cared for and yet not pressured.

That brings us to sales. "We see you bought a new iPad last month and wanted to let you know we're having a 40% discount on iPad and iPhone accessories this week. Here are a few items that will work with the tablet you bought." What better way to capitalize on a customer's slowly building apathy after the sale? We all know when the latest and greatest comes out, we feel compelled to buy it. The "buy glow" fades, however, and the perfect solution is a new accessory. New games coming out for a PS3, the next size up for kids' clothes or an electric screwdriver that follows that new drill are helpful and timely suggestions. The great thing is that these don't even need to be your own customers! You can acquire this information from any number of demographic sources and when your competition isn't serving their customers adequately, you will be standing by with the service they will appreciate. If you're familiar with the classic "Miracle on 34th Street" you will remember the scene where Santa Claus advised a Macy's customer that the toy they were seeking was in stock at Gimble's, much to the horror of the Macy's staff. The customer, however, responded with gratitude at the generosity of information and became even more loyal to Macy's because of it.

"Tell us how we're doing…" is an invitation for what is probably the most valuable information any company can have—criticism. This is an impersonal method of letting customers voice their opinion about their buying experience; an opportunity that can actually reduce your customer service headaches. The very people you're trying to make happy are telling you what you're doing wrong. What's that worth? Potentially the future of your company, that's what. Were they able to find the merchandise they were searching? Was the checkout experience simple and fast? Did they receive the product on a timely basis and were any defects readily resolved? Then, the golden question; will they be recommending your company to their friends? Some companies are afraid to let customer input have too much effect on how they conduct their business. They fear criticism instead of embracing it. Always acknowledge their comments, favorable or otherwise. If their experience was negative, you have a great opportunity to turn the situation around. Once they've vented a bit they will generally come around to your point of view if you put the time and effort in. After all, their decision to do business with you was voluntary. By enlisting the customer in a positive, inclusive manner, you make them part of the solution and they feel appeased and rewarded for their efforts. These are the customers that will stay with you for life.

Asking a customer to list their birthday lets you send them a birthday card on the big day. But it also tells you how old they are and that lets you suggest products or services they may be interested in. One brilliant marketer of this information is AARP. They issue inexpensive cards, negotiate discounts for members and then use the demographic information to try to sell you everything from health care to insurance to new cars to reverse mortgages. Yet AARP members feel cared for simply because their membership card will get them a 10% discount at their next stay at Holiday Inn. Do you really suppose they are the only group who enjoys such a privilege?

It's a good idea to build some sort of loyalty program into your cost of doing business. Your customer feels special and you have invaluable data. Perhaps you're not selling life insurance, such as AARP, but if your customer matches their demographic, they may wish to co-sponsor events with you or advertise quietly on your site. How does this help you beyond a little ad revenue? What if you're selling Hoverounds – the mobility scooter? Getting access to the AARP mailing list through a combined promotion is worth millions. To the customer you look like a respected, trustworthy source and to your bottom line, you look like a genius; all due to the obvious sponsorship of a respected brand such as AARP.

Zappos, the online shoe outlet offers free return shipping on any order. Don't you imagine they've built the cost of that shipping into the prices they charge on shoes? Absolutely; but it makes them look very customer-friendly and the customers are paying for the privilege! Returning a pair of shoes is as easy as visiting their website, logging in and a list of your purchases comes up. You click on the menu next to the pair of shoes you don't want and select "Returning." No questions asked unless you care to offer an explanation. The only thing you are asked is whether you'd like to generate your return slip now, or have it emailed to you. If email is selected, it's generated immediately and already waiting in your inbox. You take the slip, your shoes, and head for a UPS shipping station at the grocery store or drugstore and hand it over. It's as simple as that.

Are you taking advantage of the checkout experience for your business? Do you offer ancillary or related items for the upsell? If you're not, or if you're doing it badly, you're missing out on generating a caring consumer experience. For example, let's say you've bought Little Johnny the newest electronic gadget for Christmas. After ripping open the box, Johnny asks for the required AA batteries and that's when you realize that they weren't packaged with the device. There's a happy moment, ruined. Using conscientious customer service, the retailer would have known batteries weren't included and would have suggested you include some at the time of purchase.

Let's say you sell paper products. Why not offer your customers a free app that lets them build a shopping list? Naturally, your app will be liberally sprinkled with names and images of your products and maybe some recipes that involve messy eating—like barbecued ribs or lobster. You just happen to sell paper towel and lobster bibs, right?

Or perhaps you have a restaurant and you offer an app that lets the customer pre-order carry-out as they leave work. You've simplified their life and become a part of their normal routine all at the same time. The other advantage is that you can offer a "fried chicken special" and save on your butcher bill by buying in an intelligently-predicted bulk purchase.

You're a security company and you offer a free app to customers that lets them turn on lights in their home remotely or clocks when the kids come home from school. You're an airline who sends customers a weather report from the city of their destination. You're the hotel who sends guests coupons from local tourist sites when a reservation is made.

Customer goodwill will carry you through the many glitches that your relationship will always encounter. It's like the police interviewing your neighbor about the crime they're investigating. If you've used goodwill your neighbor will say, "Oh, Mr. Jones couldn't possibly have done that. He's such a nice, helpful, neighborly fellow. You've got the wrong guy."

If you've never taken the time to introduce yourself to the neighbor he's likely to say, "I don't know, maybe he could have done it. Always kept to himself, you know? Sort of suspicious fellow."

What kind of neighbor do you want to be?

CHAPTER 13

The Power of the Sequential Subconscious

This concept may be best explained if applied practically.

Dr. Lothar von Blenk-Schmidt may not be a household name, but his story is one worth remembering. A highly intelligent German engineer, Dr. Blenk-Schmidt found himself interned in a Russian prisoner-of-war camp during World War II. His daily survival depended his being able to mine at least 300 lbs. of coal each day from the local mine. If prisoners were too weak to accomplish this, their already insufficient rations were cut. Obviously, this was a slow process that could only end at the cemetery.

Dr. Blenk-Schmidt understood the power of his subconscious and forced his mind to envision himself living in Los Angeles and driving down Wilshire Blvd., a highly impractical scenario for a man who must mine 300 lbs. of coal each day to survive. Daily and nightly he built this vision so strongly that eventually he determined his own fate. Leaving out the "how it happened" suffice it to say that yes, indeed, one day thereafter he was chauffeured down Wilshire Blvd. and married the woman he had also included in his dreams.

Dr. Blenk-Schmidt survived because his subconscious took control of his life and at every opportunity, it made the decision and took the option that would eventually lead him to Wilshire Blvd. It was a process of continual selection; just as certain as a motorist who continues to turn left will eventually find himself driving in circles.

While this is an extreme example, the same sort of goal-oriented thinking can be instrumental in guiding your customers through a sales sequence.

Consumers are, in many ways, insecure. They have been programmed to believe over their lifetime through media exposure that they are always somehow lacking. They are too fat, too ugly, have bad breath, bad taste, bad judgement and their greatest sins can be overcome if they would simply follow the announcer's guidance. Buy the diet pill, the toothpaste, the insurance policy or whatever the product and they can be redeemed and made once again acceptable.

Thus, the advertiser is planting a subconscious need in the mind of the consumer, and then solving the problem for them.

While you may protest that this seems a bit Machiavellian in approach, the truth is that consumers want to be told what to do. It stems from their response as young children; to do whatever Mom, the teacher, the police, or the minister tells them to do. And why? Because the police, et al will always be doing what's best for the consumer/person. "It's for your own good," they are told.

Thus, when they follow the rules, they feel the better for it. So, in a sense, you are making them happier and more contented with their purchase by showing them the following four concepts—the roots of walking a consumer through a sales sequence.

1. Here's what the product is

2. Here's what the product can do for you

3. Here's how I know that's true

4. Here's your next step so that you, too, can realize the pride of accomplishment or ownership

While these four rules are easy to remember in concept, they may come a bit more disguised in reality. Make a habit of watching television commercials and see if you can pick out the sequenced approach. Once you develop this sort of "x-ray vision" consider how you might use it to help your own customers. Are they left puzzled as you introduce your company or service? Are they unsure what to do next? Are they making continual left turns instead of following the map you need them to see?

Your role as a successful business person is to leave your customer fulfilled. That gives them a positive experience and keeps them faithful to you. Consider yourself an evangelist of your profession or field. Show them how you can make their life better and achieve their version of Wilshire Blvd.

Your success lies in helping your customer realize his own.

* * * * *

Now you have the magic bullet called "potential" in your own hands; except that you now know there is no magic to it at all. How will you use it? How and when will you "Flip the Switch"?

www.ingramcontent.com/pod-product-compliance
Lightning Source LLC
Chambersburg PA
CBHW051815170526
45167CB00005B/2031